A Place for Me

A Place for Me

Bernard J. Weiss
Senior Author
Reading and Linguistics

Eldonna L. Evertts
Language Arts

Susan B. Cruikshank
Reading and Language Arts

Loreli Olson Steuer
Reading and Linguistics

Lyman C. Hunt
General Editor—Satellite Books

Holt
Basic
Reading

Level 7
HOLT, RINEHART AND WINSTON, PUBLISHERS
New York ● Toronto ● Mexico City ● London ● Sydney ● Tokyo

ISBN 0-03-061388-4
8910 071 987654

Acknowledgments:

Grateful acknowledgment is given to the following authors and publishers:

Allyn and Bacon, Inc., for "Mister Rabbit" accompaniment from *This Is Music*, Book 1, by William R. Sur, Adeline McCall, William R. Fisher, and Mary R. Tolbert. Copyright © 1967, 1962, by Allyn and Bacon, Inc. Used by permission.

Bradbury Press, Inc., for "The Small Lot" adapted from *A Small Lot* by Eros Keith. Copyright © 1968 by Eros Keith, published by Bradbury Press, Inc. Used by permission.

The Dial Press, for "Maybe a Monster" adapted from *Maybe a Monster* by Martha Alexander. Copyright © 1968 by Martha Alexander and used by permission of the publisher, The Dial Press.

E. P. Dutton & Co., Inc., for "Park Bench" from the book *Rhymes About The City* by Marchette Chute. Copyright 1946 by Marchette Chute, and used by permission of the publisher, E. P. Dutton & Co., Inc.

Grosset & Dunlap, Inc., for "Save My Place," adapted from *Save My Place* by Russell Hoban and Lillian Hoban. Copyright © 1967 by Grosset & Dunlap, Inc. Used by permission.

Harcourt Brace Jovanovich, Inc., and Curtis Brown, Ltd., for "An old silent pond . . ." from *Cricket Songs: Japanese Haiku*, translated and copyrighted © 1964 by Harry Behn. Used by permission.

Holt, Rinehart and Winston, Publishers for "Sunny Days," from *Kim's Place* by Lee Bennett Hopkins. Copyright © 1974 by Lee Bennett Hopkins. For, "Around the Corner" from *Just Around the Corner* by Leland B. Jacobs. Copyright © 1964 by Leland B. Jacobs. Used by permission.

Houghton Mifflin Company and World's Work Ltd., for "Too Much Noise" adapted from *Too Much Noise* by Ann McGovern. Copyright © 1967 by Ann McGovern and Simms Taback. Used by permission.

Simon & Schuster, Inc., for "The Grass," from *Miracles* by Richard Lewis. Copyright © 1966 by Richard Lewis. Used by permission.

Henry Z. Walck, Inc., for "Sing a Song of People," from *Songs of the City* by Lois Lenski and Clyde Robert. Copyright © 1956 by Lois Lenski. Used by permission of the author.

Art Credits:

Ethel Gold, pages 10 – 24 and 86 – 101
Peter Cross, page 25
Tim and Greg Hildebrandt, pages 120 – 126 and 128
Len Ebert, pages 26 – 32
Lionel Kalish, pages 33 – 43 and 104 – 117
Eros Keith, pages 44 – 57
Sven Lindman, pages 58, 156 (career graphics)
Joe Veno, pages 58 – 59 and 156 – 157
Michael O'Reilly, page 66
Diane de Groat, pages 67 – 81, 103, 118 – 119, and 142 – 143

George Senty, photos: pages 72 – 80
Ruth Sanderson, page 82
Howard Darden, pages 83 and 158
Marie Michal, page 102
Ric Del Rossi, page 103
Bill Morrison, page 127
Frank Riley, pages 129 – 141
Zena Bernstein, pages 144 – 155
Cover art by James Endicott
Unit Opener art by Nancy Schill

Photo Credits:

p. 58 top, Ken Wittenberg; bottom, HRW Photo by Russell Dian. p. 59 Ken Wittenberg. pp. 60 – 65 Katerina Thomas. pp. 72 – 80 George Senty. p. 156 top, Burt Glinn/Magnum, bottom, John Running/Stock Boston. p. 157 top, T. Nebbia/dpi; bottom, Amwest.

Table of Contents

UNIT TWO
QUIET ROADS

BUSY STREETS

Sunny Days

Mile-long skyscrapers are my trees.
The subway's *whoosh,* my summer-breeze.

The hydrant is my swimming pool
Where all my friends keep real cool.

The city is the place to be.
The city is the place for me.

—Lee Bennett Hopkins

Teddy's Window

PART ONE
Three Blue Trucks

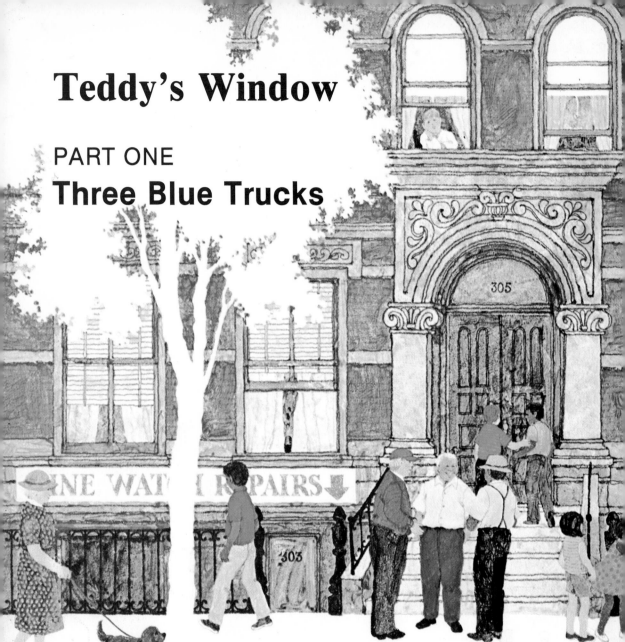

Teddy was sick.
He didn't like it.
He couldn't play.
He couldn't eat.
And he couldn't go out.

Teddy looked out his window.
He saw some boys and girls.
He saw some boys and girls play.
But he couldn't go out.
And they couldn't come in.

Teddy looked out the window
and saw the people.
They went up and down the street.
But not Teddy!
Teddy was sick.

Some people went into the stores.
But not Teddy!
He couldn't go out.
Teddy was sick.
And he didn't like it.

Night came.
But Teddy was up.
He was sick and couldn't sleep.
Teddy looked out the window.
He looked up and down the street.

No one was on the street.
No one was in the stores.
No cars came down the street.
But Teddy did see some blue trucks.
They came down his street.

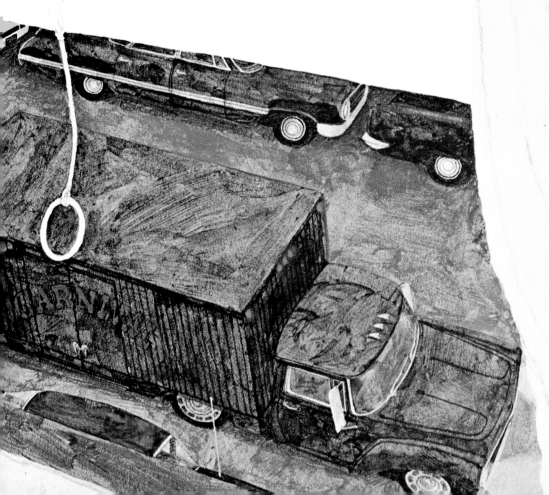

Teddy saw signs on the trucks.
The signs said, "Carnival."
The trucks went on down the street.
They went into a big lot.

Teddy saw the lot from his window.
He saw the carnival people.
He saw the trucks stop.
The carnival people went to sleep.
And Teddy went to sleep.

PART TWO

Come One—Come All

Morning came.
Teddy looked out the window.
He saw the carnival.
A big sign said,
"Come One—Come All.
Come to the Carnival!"

18

COME ONE - COME ALL
COME TO THE
CARNIVAL!

"Mother!" said Teddy.
"I want to go to the carnival!"

"But you can't go out," said Mother.
"You are sick, Teddy.
You can't go to the carnival."

Teddy looked out the window.
He wanted to see the carnival.

Teddy saw a boy.
The boy came down the street.
The boy saw Teddy and stopped.

"Did you see the carnival?" Teddy asked.

"See it!" said the boy.
"I'm in the carnival."

"Then you can see all of it," said Teddy.
"I can't see one show.
I'm sick.
I can't go out.
All I can do is look out the window."

"But you can see one show," said the boy.
And he ran up the street.

The boy came back down the street.
He came back with a monkey.

"I'm back," said the boy.
"I'm back with the show.
My monkey will do tricks for you."

Teddy looked out his window.
And the monkey did some tricks.

"What a monkey!" said Teddy.

All the boys and girls on the street stopped.
The monkey did the tricks again.

"What a show!" said the boys and girls.

"It is my show!" said the boy.
"I'm in it!"

The boy said good-by.
And he ran back to the carnival.

"What a morning!" said Teddy.
He wanted to go back to sleep.

Mother looked at Teddy.
"It was a **good** morning!" she said.
"You did go to the carnival, didn't you?"

"No, I didn't," said Teddy.
"The carnival came to me."

Changing Words

1. The boy ____ a monkey.   **ran**

2. The frog ____ swim.   **can**

3. The cat ____ up the tree.   **man**

4. Are you ____ at me?   **mad**

5. The ____ sleeps here.   **had**

     hat

1. Look at the ____ bear.   **pig**

2. ____ you see the carnival?   **big**

3. My brother ____ from me.   **dig**

4. I saw a cow and a ____ .   **did**

5. The monkey ran to ____ .   **him**

     hid

Not Yet, Clarita

Annie DeCaprio

Clarita's big brother has a car.
Clarita likes Juan's car.
She likes to go places in it.

One day Juan said to Clarita,
"I'm going to the store.
Do you want to go with me?"

"Yes!" said Clarita.
"I do! I do!
But what do you want at the store?
Can you tell me?"

Juan said, "I can tell you.
But not yet, Clarita!"

Juan and Clarita went down the street.

"Do you see the store yet?" asked Clarita.

"No," said Juan. "Not yet, Clarita."

"I see a sign," Clarita said.
"I see the sign for the store.
Stop, Juan!
Stop the car!"

Clarita and Juan went into the store.

"I see what I want," Juan said.
"I'll go get it.
Where will I find you?"

"I want to look at the pets," said Clarita.
"I'll be with the pets."

Clarita looked at the pets.
She saw some dogs.
She saw a little cat.
She saw lots of fish.
And she saw Juan.

"Did you find what you wanted?"
asked Clarita.

"No," said Juan.
"Not yet, Clarita."

30

Then Juan said,
"I saw you look at the goldfish.
Do you want a goldfish?"

"Yes," said Clarita.
"I do want a goldfish.
Someday I'll get one."

"I'll get one for you," said Juan.
"Happy Name Day, Clarita!"

Clarita and Juan went back to the car.

"What did you want, Juan?" asked Clarita.
"Can you tell me now?"

"Yes," said Juan.
"I wanted to find out what **you** wanted.
It's your Name Day, Clarita.
I wanted you to have a happy day!"

And, for Clarita, it was a happy Name Day.

Drills

There's an awful rumble
Outside my door
Like the dentist's drill
Only much, much more!

It seems to make
My own jaws shake.
I guess the sidewalk
Has a toothache.

—Maltier Chauncey

33

The Grumpiest Man

PART ONE
Stop That Noise!

My house was in a big city.
I liked the city.
I liked the people on my street.
All but one man!
He was the grumpiest man on the street.

34

That man didn't like people.
He didn't like cats.
He didn't like dogs.
He didn't like cars.
He didn't like trucks.
They all made noise.
And that man didn't like noise.

35

The people on my street go to work
in the morning.
But not that man!
He goes to work at night.
And in the morning he likes to sleep.

The boys and girls went out to play.

"Stop that noise," said the man.

A man came to work on the street.

"I can't sleep with all that noise,"
said the man.

But the noise didn't stop.
And the man couldn't sleep.
He was the grumpiest man
on the street.

PART TWO

The Earmuffs

One day Daddy and I went to the store.
Daddy wanted to get me a game.

We looked at the games.
I didn't see one I liked.

"I don't want a game," I said.

Then I saw some earmuffs.
And that made my day.
I had to laugh.

"Daddy," I said.
"Here is what I want."

"What do you want earmuffs for?"
asked Daddy.

"I want them for that man
who sleeps all morning," I said.

"What will that man do
with the earmuffs?" asked Daddy.

"He can put them on," I said.
"The earmuffs will stop the noise.
Then he can sleep."

Daddy laughed.
"I will get them for you," he said.

Daddy and I went up the street.
The man was at his window.

"Stop that noise," he said to some boys.

"Here!" we said.
"We got some earmuffs for you.
Put them on and the noise will stop."

The man put on the earmuffs.
Then he laughed.
And then he went back to sleep.

The noise didn't stop.
The boys and girls went on playing.
The cars went up and down the street.
But no one came to the window.
No one said, "Stop that noise."
And no one said, "That man is
the grumpiest man on the street.

The Small Lot
Eros Keith

PART ONE
The Lot

In a big city there was
a small lot.
In the lot there was a tree.
Jay and Bob liked to play
in the tree in the lot.

The two boys made up games
to play in the tree.

One morning a man and his dog came
to the lot.
The man stopped and said to his dog,
"I can put a pet store here."

He looked at the small lot again.
He looked and looked.

"No," he said.
"That lot is too small."

That morning in the lot,
Jay and Bob played pet store.

49

A man and a woman came to the lot.
They stopped and looked at it.

"We can put a flower store here,"
said the man.

"I'll put a big window in the store,"
he said.

"That lot is too small
for a flower store," said the woman.

Then Jay and Bob played flower store
in the lot.

PART TWO
A Small Park

One morning three women came
to the lot.

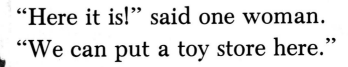

"Here it is!" said one woman.
"We can put a toy store here."

"Not here!" said a woman.
"That lot is too small for a toy store."

The women went on down the street.

That afternoon in the lot,
Jay and Bob played toy store.

One day Bob said to Jay,
"What if someone comes and says
that the lot is **not** too small?
Then what will we do?"

Jay went home.
And Bob went home.
That night the boys couldn't sleep.

In the morning Jay and Bob didn't go
to the lot.
They went down the street.
They came back with a bench
and some flowers.

That afternoon the man and his dog
came back to the lot.
The man looked at the lot
again and again.

The man saw the bench
and the flowers.
He looked at his dog and said,
"I can't put a pet store here.
It's a park!"

The man looked at the lot again.
Then he went home with his dog.

Jay and Bob laughed and went on playing.

On Busy Streets

It's morning in the city! The streets are very busy. They are filled with cars and people. Lots of people! The people are hurrying to work and to school.

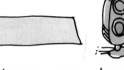

City stores are busy stores. Some of the stores are already open. People stop at the stores on their way to work. They say, "Good morning!" to Mr. Rodriguez. He owns the market on the corner.

They ask Miss Nuberg, "What's today's lunch?" Miss Nuberg works in a delicatessen down the street. She always has something very good for the people to take with them to work.

58

Already some people are shopping for dinner. This man sells fresh fish. The fish were caught just hours ago. The people who caught the fish had to begin *their* work while it was still dark!

What's going on here? Children used to play on this street. Now the street is dug up. People stop to watch the men at work on the street.

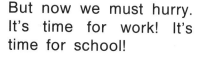

The men are busy laying a new cable. Soon the street will be like new, and the children will be able to play here again.

But now we must hurry. It's time for work! It's time for school!

59

A Good Place to Play

In a big city there was a lot.
The lot had no flowers.
It had no trees.
It had no place to sit.

People didn't like the lot.
They wanted a park there.

Here is a picture of the lot.

61

Boys and girls made pictures of the park.
They put in places to play games.
They put in benches to sit on.

Here is the picture that one girl made.
Do you see the places to play?
Do you see the benches?

People looked at the pictures.
They liked what they saw.
They all went to work on the lot.
Now they have a park!

The boys and girls like the park.
It is not a big park.
But now they have a place to play.
And now they have a place to sit.

What Do You Mean?

park   lot   back   show   place

1. The boy ran _____ to his house.
   I like to sleep on my _____ .

2. I like my pet a _____ .
   The house is on a big _____ .

3. We play in the _____ .
   Daddy will _____ the car.

4. Jill, _____ me where the pictures are.
   We will have a pet _____ .

5. There is no _____ to play here.
   The toys are all in _____ .

Semantics. Have the children read the words at the top of the page and discuss several meanings for each. Find the word that fits in each pair of sentences.

A Place for Fred

PART ONE

Country Frog

"I'm sick of it here," said Fred.
"I'm sick of water.
I'm sick of animals.
The country is no place for me!"

"I know what I'll do, Goldie," said Fred.
"I'll go to the city.
I won't see a lot of animals there.
But I will see a lot of people.
It's time I went to the city.
The city is the place for me."

"The city!" said Goldie.
"You won't like it there.
It's no place for a frog.
What can you do in the city?"

"I'll find work," said Fred.
"People will show me what to do.
Come with me, Goldie.
What a time we can have in the city."

69

"A goldfish in the city!"
said Goldie.
"No, Fred.
The country is the place for animals.
The country is the place for me.
But you go if you want to.
And have a good time."

"Then it's good-by, Goldie,"
said Fred.
"If you get to the city, look me up."

And with that, Fred went
down the road to find the city.

"City people, here I come!" he said.

PART TWO
City Frog

Fred got to the city that afternoon.

"Look at the people," he said.
"I was right.
I may be a country frog.
But the city is the place for me.
Now where do I go from here?"

Fred saw a man
on a bench.
Fred got right up
on the bench.
"Hello there," he said.
"I'm from the country.
And I don't have work.
Maybe you can tell me
where to find work."

The man went right on
reading.

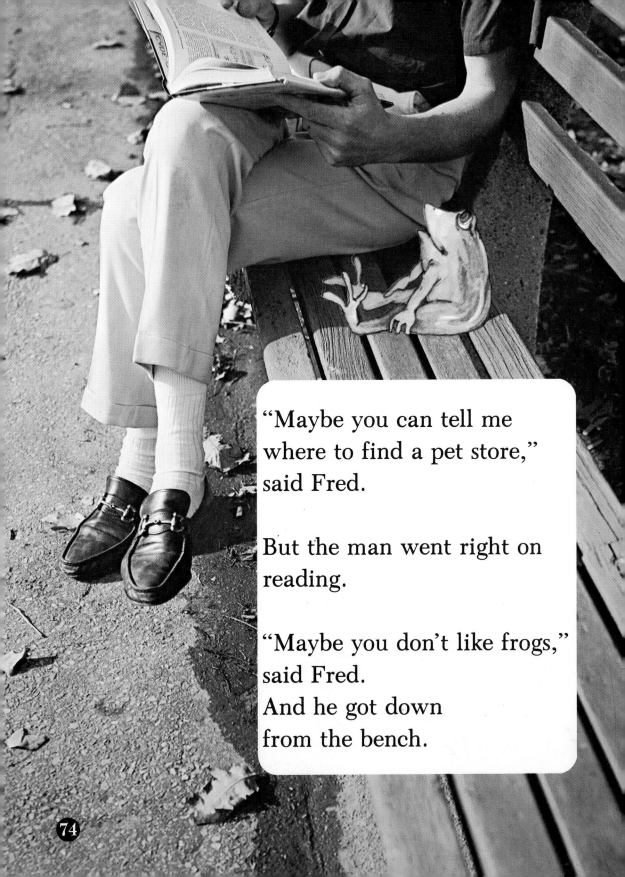

"Maybe you can tell me
where to find a pet store,"
said Fred.

But the man went right on
reading.

"Maybe you don't like frogs,"
said Fred.
And he got down
from the bench.

Then Fred saw a store with lots of people.
"I'll go in here and ask for work," he said.

Fred went in.
"Hello," he said to a woman.
"I'm Fred.
I'm looking for work.
Maybe you have some work I can do."

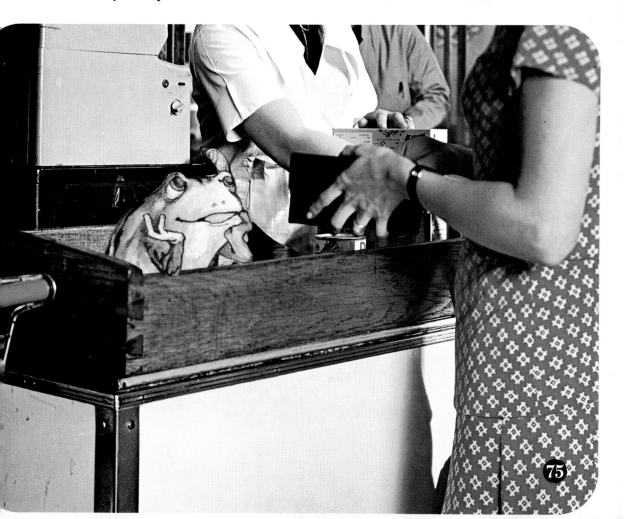

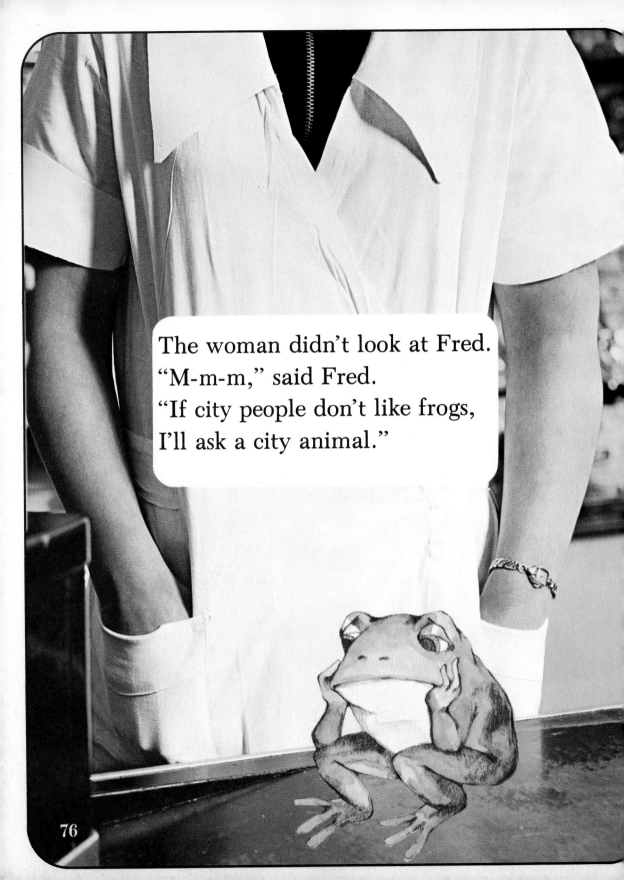

The woman didn't look at Fred.
"M-m-m," said Fred.
"If city people don't like frogs,
I'll ask a city animal."

PART THREE
Fred Finds a Home

Fred went back out to the street.
A car came down the street.
When Fred saw it,
he jumped.

"M-m-m," said Fred.
"I'll have to look
where I'm going.
People in cars can't see frogs."

Then Fred saw a girl
with a big dog.

"Hello," said Fred to the dog.
"Do you work here in the city?"

The dog didn't look at Fred.
And Fred went on down the street.

Then a boy came up the street
and saw Fred.
"A frog," said the boy.
"I love frogs.
You can come home with me."

But the boy's home was not
in the city.
It was in the country.

That night Fred was in a car,
going right back to the country.

When Goldie saw Fred, she said,
"You came back, Fred.
You came back to the country.
The country is the place for you!"

Fred looked at Goldie and the trees
and the flowers.

"You may be right, Goldie," he said.
"You may be right."

And into the water he jumped.

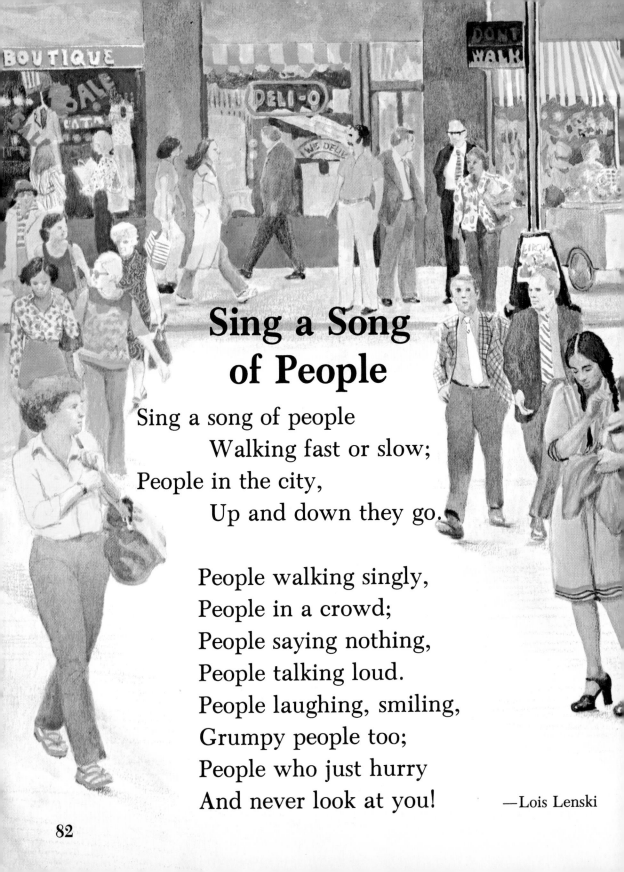

Sing a Song
of People

Sing a song of people
    Walking fast or slow;
People in the city,
    Up and down they go.

People walking singly,
People in a crowd;
People saying nothing,
People talking loud.
People laughing, smiling,
Grumpy people too;
People who just hurry
And never look at you!

—Lois Lenski

Stringing Words

Jay	wanted	games
Clarita	liked	flowers
Daddy	made	books

1. ____ was sick.

2. Teddy ____ trucks.

3. Mother saw ____ .

4. Kate ____ toys.

5. ____ went home.

6. Jill wants ____ .

7. Juan ____ that book.

8. Tim likes ____ .

QUIET ROADS

The Grass

The grass seems to dance.
It seems to walk,
It seems to talk,
It seems to like to
Have you walk on it,
And play with it, too.

It seems to be stronger than you or I.

—Warren Cardwell, Age 8

Amy
PART ONE
Lonely

Amy's street was a good place to live.
There were three houses on the street.
One house was big.
One house was small.
And one was Amy's house.

There were flowers and trees
where Amy lived.
There were places to play.
And there were boys and girls
to play with.
But Amy was lonely.

Amy's big brother had a friend.
His friend lived in the small house.
Amy's little sister had two friends.
They lived in the big house.

Amy's mother and daddy had friends.
They came to Amy's house.
But Amy didn't have a friend.
She was lonely.

PART TWO
Good News

One afternoon Amy's brother had news.

"I have some good news," he said.
"Brad's dog had puppies.
Brown and white puppies!"

"Did you see the new puppies?"
asked Amy.

"Yes," said Amy's brother.
"One is all brown.
Two are white.
And three are brown and white."

"I want to see the puppies,"
said Amy.

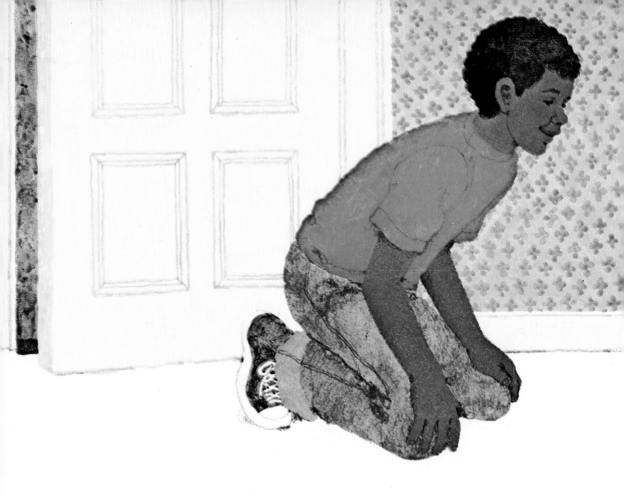

Amy ran to Brad's house.

"Will you show me the new puppies?"
she asked Brad.

"Yes," said Brad.
"I'll show them to you.
But you can't pick them up.
They are sleeping."

Amy went into the house.
There were the puppies.
Amy wanted to pick them up.
But she couldn't.
The puppies were sleeping.
They were all in one place.
All but the little brown and white one.
He looked lonely.

Amy looked at the sleeping puppies.
Then she said,
"I want to pick you up.
But I won't.
Good-by little puppies."

And Amy went home.

PART THREE

New Friends

Amy went to see the puppies again.
She liked all of them.
But she loved the little one.
And the little puppy loved Amy.
He ran to Amy when she came in.
When she went home,
he wanted to go, too.

One day Amy went
to see the puppies.
They were not there!

"Where are the puppies?"
she asked Brad.

"The puppies are gone," he said.
"The house is too small.
It's too small for all the puppies.
Daddy had to find homes for them."

"The puppies are gone!" said Amy.
"I won't get to play with them again."

Amy ran home.

"Mother," said Amy.
"The puppies are gone!
I can't play with them."

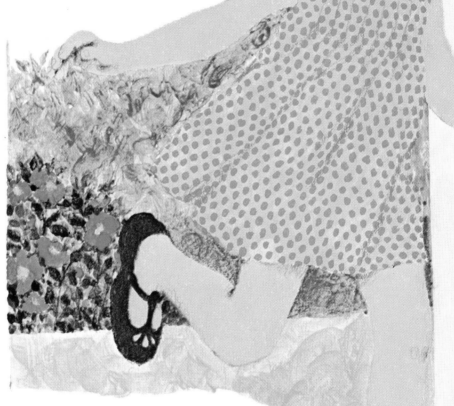

"Not all the puppies are gone,"
said Mother.
"Come and see what I have for you."

Amy went into the house.
There was the little brown and
white puppy.

"Is that puppy for me?"
asked Amy.

"Yes, he is," said Mother.
"Daddy and I wanted you to have
a friend to play with."

Amy made a good home for the puppy.
She made a place for him to eat.
And she made a place for him to sleep.
She played with him.
They were good friends.

The boys and girls on Amy's street
came to see the puppy.
They came to see Amy, too.
Now Amy had a lot of friends.
She was not lonely again.

Puppy Work

I had a pair of bright green shoes;
I only wore them Sundays.
My puppy chewed on them one night,
And now I wear them Mondays.

Stringing Words

We	sleep	at night.
You	play	in the morning.
They	read	all the time.
	eat	in the afternoon.

Did	we	sleep	at night?
Will	you	play	in the morning?
Can	they	read	all the time?
Do		eat	in the afternoon?

Sentence Patterns. Let the children choose a word or words from each column to form a sentence. At the bottom of the page, point out how the words in the first column can be added to change the sentences to questions.

Too Much Noise

Ann McGovern

PART ONE
All That Noise

Peter was an old man
who lived in an old, old house.

There was too much noise
in Peter's house.
The bed made noise.
The door made noise.
And the window made noise.
Peter didn't like all that noise.

Peter went to see an old wise man.
"What can I do?"
Peter asked the wise man.
"My house makes too much noise.
My bed makes noise.
My door makes noise.
And my window makes noise."

"Get a cow," the wise man said.

"What good is a cow?" asked Peter.

But Peter did what the wise man said.
He got a cow.

The cow said, "Moo. Moo."
The bed made noise.
The door made noise.
And the window made noise.

"Too much noise," said Peter.
"Too much noise."

Peter went back to the wise man.

"Get a burro," said the wise man.

"What good is a burro?" asked Peter.

But Peter did what the wise man said.
He got a burro.

The burro said, "Hee-Haw."

The cow said, "Moo. Moo."

The bed made noise.
The door made noise.
And the window made noise.

"Too much noise," said Peter.
And he went back to the wise man.

"Get a dog," the wise man said.
"And get a cat, too."

"What good is a dog?" asked Peter.
"And what good is a cat?"

But Peter did what the wise man said.
He got a dog and a cat.

The dog said, "Woof. Woof."

The cat said, "Mee-ow. Mee-ow."

The burro said, "Hee-Haw."

The cow said, "Moo. Moo."

The bed made noise.
The door made noise.
And the window made noise.

"Too much noise," said Peter.
And out the door he went.

PART TWO
A Quiet Noise

Peter went back to the wise man.
"You told me to get a cow," said Peter.
"All day the cow says, 'Moo. Moo.'
You told me to get a burro.
All day the burro says, 'Hee-Haw.'
You told me to get a dog and a cat.
All day the dog says 'Woof. Woof.'
All day the cat says, Mee-ow. Mee-ow.'
I did what you told me," said Peter.

"Now what can I do?" asked Peter.
"There is too much noise
in my house."

"Let the cow go," said the wise man.
"Let the burro go.
Let the dog go.
And let the cat go."

Peter went home.
He let the cow go.
He let the burro go.
He let the dog go.
And he let the cat go.

Now there was no cow to say,
"Moo! Moo!"
and no burro to say, "Hee-Haw!"
and no dog to say, "Woof! Woof!"
and no cat to say, "Mee-ow! Mee-ow!"

The bed made noise.
The door made noise.
The window made noise.

"What a quiet noise," said Peter.
"And what a quiet house."

Peter got into his bed
and went to sleep.

Had a Cat

1. I had a cat and the cat pleased me,

I fed my cat by yon-der tree;

Cat goes fid-dle - i - fee._____

2. I had a dog and the dog pleased me,
   I fed my dog by yonder tree;
   Dog goes bow-wow, bow-wow.
   Cat goes fiddle-i-fee.

3. I had a cow and the cow pleased me,
   I fed my cow by yonder tree;
   Cow goes moo, moo, moo, moo.
   Dog goes bow-wow, bow-wow.
   Cat goes fiddle-i-fee.

Maybe a Monster

Martha Alexander

I'm going to make a trap.
What will I trap?
Maybe a monster!

Where can I put a monster?
I'll have to make a house for it.

Maybe the monster will be big.
I'll have to make a big house.

Maybe the monster will have two heads.
I'll have to make a place for the heads.

What if fire comes out of the monster?
I'll have to make a place for the fire
to come out.

Maybe the monster will have a big tail.
I'll have to make a place for the tail.

Maybe the monster will have big wings.
I'll make a place for the wings.

Now I'll go and trap the monster.
A monster with two heads and a tail.
A monster with wings and fire!
I'll have to get some water.
Then I can put out the fire.
Now I'll get the monster.

"Look what I got!"

"What is that?"   "Can't you see?
It's a rabbit house."

Around the Corner

Just around the corner,
You just might meet
A happy young dinosaur
Walking in the street.

—Leland B. Jacobs

127

A Sentence Grows

Jim is a man.

Jim Parks is a man.

Jim Parks is a big man.

Jim Parks is a big man

who likes to eat.

Jim Parks is a big man

who likes to eat a lot

of cookies.

Sentence Modifiers. Have each sentence read and discuss how it
differs from the previous sentence. Which sentence tells the most?

The Flower Kitten

Kitty's house was in town.
Kitty liked to live in town.
And she liked Jenny.

One day, Kitty wanted
to see the country.
"Mee-ow," said Kitty.

Jenny was making cookies.
But she looked at Kitty.
"Do you want to go out?"
she asked.
"Mee-ow!" said Kitty again.

130

Kitty ran out.
She ran to the street.
Then she stopped.
Jenny said not to go into the street.

"Mee-ow!" said Kitty.
But she did not go into the street.

Kitty looked and looked.
Kitty turned right.
She went down the street.

Then Kitty saw an open truck.
She saw flowers in the truck.
She jumped up into the back of the truck.

Kitty liked it in the back of the truck.
She liked the flowers she saw there.

"Flowers are in the country," thought Kitty.
"I am in the country!"

Then the driver jumped into the truck.
Kitty was very quiet.
She did not see Kitty in the flowers.

The truck went down the street.
It came to a sign.
The sign said, "STOP."
The truck stopped.

134

Then the truck turned right.
It was on a new street.
The truck went down that street.

The truck came to some stores.
The driver stopped the truck.
She went into a store with a flower.
Kitty did not like to see the flower go.

Then the driver got back into the truck.
Again, the truck went on down the street.
Kitty looked out of the truck.
"Mee-ow! Mee-ow!" she said, very quietly.
Kitty liked all the flowers.
Wasn't the country nice.
Kitty didn't want to go back to town.

Again, the truck came to a sign.
The sign said, "STOP."
The truck stopped.

Again, the truck turned right.
It was on a new street.
Again, the truck stopped at a store.
Again, the driver went into a store
with a flower.

Then the driver saw Kitty in the back
of the truck.
Kitty did not look at all like a flower.
No flower looked at all like Kitty.
So the driver saw Kitty.
"Hello," she said.

"Mee-ow," said Kitty.

The truck went down the street.
"STOP," said a sign.
The truck stopped.
Then the truck turned right.

18 WATER ST.

Kitty looked out of the truck.
There was Jenny!
"I am back in town," thought Kitty.

Jenny was making a sign to the truck.
The driver stopped the truck.

"Hello, Mrs. Gold!" said Jenny.
"I want a flower."

"Hello, Jenny!" said Mrs. Gold.
"Here's a flower for you.
A very nice flower!
And here's Kitty.
She jumped into my truck."

Kitty jumped out of the truck.
She and the flower went into the house
with Jenny.

"Some of the country is here in the flower," Jenny said.

Kitty looked at the flower. She saw some of the country in the flower.

"I am back in town," thought Kitty. "But some of the country is right here with Jenny."

Mister Rabbit

1. Mis-ter Rab-bit, Mis-ter Rab-bit,

your hair is might-y gray.

Yes, kind sir, it was made that way. —

Refrain

Ev-ery lit-tle soul's gon-na shine, shine. —

Ev-ery lit-tle soul's gon-na shine, shine. —

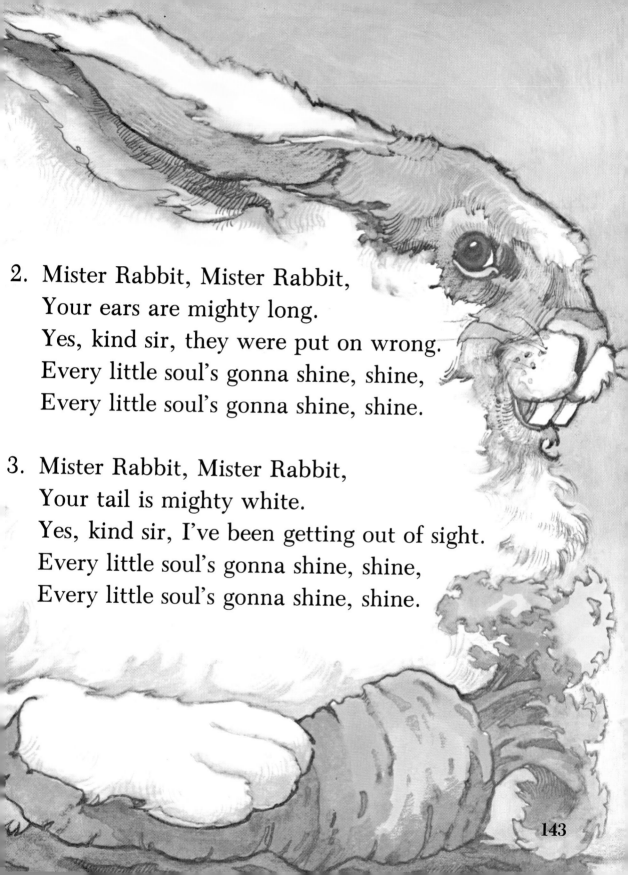

2. Mister Rabbit, Mister Rabbit,
   Your ears are mighty long.
   Yes, kind sir, they were put on wrong.
   Every little soul's gonna shine, shine,
   Every little soul's gonna shine, shine.

3. Mister Rabbit, Mister Rabbit,
   Your tail is mighty white.
   Yes, kind sir, I've been getting out of sight.
   Every little soul's gonna shine, shine,
   Every little soul's gonna shine, shine.

Save My Place
(A Play)
Russell and Lillian Hoban

The animals in the play

Rabbit	Bird
Mouse	Squirrel
Raccoon	Big Frog
Chipmunk	Three Little Frogs

145

Time.	Night
Place.	By the water. (A rabbit sits and looks at the water. A mouse comes by and sees him.)

Mouse. Hello, Rabbit.
        What are you doing here?

Rabbit. I'm saving my place.

Mouse. Maybe I'll save a place, too.

(Mouse sits down by Rabbit.
Raccoon comes by and sees them.)

146

Raccoon. Are you saving the place
by you, Mouse?

Mouse. No. You can have it.

(Raccoon sits down by Mouse.
Chipmunk comes by and sees the animals.
Chipmunk sits down by Raccoon.)

Chipmunk: What are we doing here, Raccoon?

Raccoon: I'm saving places!

Chipmunk: It's good that I got here in time.

(Bird comes by and sees the animals.)

Bird.   Is there a place for me?

Chipmunk.   You can have the one by me.

(Bird gets in his place by Chipmunk.
Squirrel comes by and sees the animals.)

Squirrel.   May I save a place, too?

Bird.   Yes. You can save the one by me.

(Squirrel sits down by Bird.
Big Frog comes out of the water.)

Rabbit.   There he is.
It's time for the show!

(The animals are quiet.)

Big Frog.   Hello.
             My friends and I will now
             sing for you.

(Little Frogs come up out of the water.
All the frogs sing "Mister Rabbit.")

Rabbit.   That was a good show.
Did you like it, Mouse?

Mouse.   Yes, I did.

Raccoon.   I liked it, too.
Will you sing again, Big Frog?

Big Frog.   Yes. We will come back
and sing again.
It's time to go now.
Good night, friends.

(All the frogs go back into the water.)

Squirrel.   The frogs are gone.
I'm going home now.
Save my place.

(Squirrel goes home.)

Bird.   Save my place.

(Bird goes home.)

Chipmunk.   Save my place.

(Chipmunk goes home.)

Raccoon.   Save my place.

(Raccoon goes home.)

Mouse.   Save my place.

(Mouse goes home.)

Rabbit.   I'll come back in the morning
and save my place.

(Rabbit goes home to sleep.)

On Quiet Roads

COCK-A-DOODLE-DO!
COOK-A-DOODLE-DO!

Hurry up! Get out of bed! The sun is just coming up. It's early morning in the country. There's lots to do before the day is done.

Fields must be plowed and planted. Crops must be picked and put into trucks. Most farm workers use machines to help them do these jobs.

Mr. Marx drives a machine that harvests grain. Grain is used to make cereals and breads that you eat. Miss Walker drives a big tractor. It pulls a machine that ties hay into bales.

156

Do you know who else eats grain?

Many animals eat grain, too. The grain helps them to grow big and fat, like the cattle you see in these pictures.

Prize cattle are sometimes sold at auctions. People tell the auctioneer how much they are willing to pay for the cattle. The auctioneer sells the cattle to the person who will pay the most.

Cattle are raised on a special farm called a ranch. Here you see a rancher rounding up his cattle. He herds them into a fenced area called a corral.

Where would you like to work when you grow up? On a busy street in the city? Or on a quiet country road?

Sentence Signals

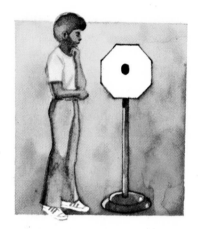  

1. My kitten likes to look out the window

2. Look what I got

3. The people like to sing

4. What time is it

5. Save me

6. Where did you go

7. Open the door

8. When did the boy get sick

Punctuation Cues. Discuss the punctuation marks and how they help in reading. Let the children select a punctuation mark for each of the eight sentences and explain the reasons for their choices.

New Words

10. Teddy's
    window
    trucks
    *Teddy**
    sick
    couldn't
    *eat**
11. *looked*
    some
    *but**
12. people
    street
13. *stores**
14. night*
    sleep
15. cars*
16. carnival
    lot
18. morning
    all
19. Mother
    *you**
    can't*

20. *wanted*
    stopped
21. show
    I'm
22. *back*
    monkey
    tricks
24. *at*
26. *yet*
    Clarita
    Clarita's
    car
    Juan's
    places
    day
    Juan
    going
27. *yes*
    tell
29. I'll
    where*
    pets
    be

30. *dogs*
    lots
    of
    fish
31. then
    someday
    happy
32. now
    it's
    your
    name
    have
34. grumpiest
    man
    that
    noise
    liked
    city*
35. *made*
36. work
39. earmuffs
    Daddy
    we

games
don't
had
laugh
40. them
    sleeps
41. put
    laughed
42. *got*
43. playing
44. small
    there
    tree*
47. *pet*
    too
48. *played*
50. woman
    flower
52. park
    women
    toy
    afternoon
54. *if*

55. *home*
56. bench
   flowers
60. *trees*
   sit
   picture
62. *pictures*
   benches
67. Fred
   country*
   frog*
   animals
68. know
   Goldie
   won't
   time
71. *road*
72. right
   may
73. hello*
   maybe
   reading
75. ask
   looking
76. *frogs*
   animal
77. *finds*

when
jumped
79. love
80. *boy's*
86. Amy
   lonely
   Amy's
   live
   were
   houses*
87. lived
88. friend
   friends
90. news
   Brad's
   puppies
   white
91. new
   brown
92. *Brad*
   pick
   sleeping
95. loved
   puppy
96. gone
   homes
100. *him*

104. *much*
   Peter
   an
   old
105. *Peter's*
   door
106. *wise*
   makes
108. moo
109. burro
110. hee-haw
111. *cat*
112. woof
   mee-ow
113. quiet
   told
114. *let*
116. *say*
120. trap
   monster
122. heads
   fire
123. *tail*
   wings
126. rabbit
129. kitten
   Kitty's

Kitty
town
130. making
132. turned
133. open
   truck
   thought
   am
134. driver
   very
136. *quietly*
   wasn't
   nice
138. *so*
140. Mrs. Gold
   here's
144. *save*
   mouse*
   raccoon
   chipmunk
   bird
   squirrel
146. *sits*
   doing
   saving
149. *gets*
151. *sing*